The Dog Food Cookbook

Easy Homemade Foods And Treats To Keep Your Dog Healthy & Happy

KATHY LARSON

Copyright © 2023 **Kathy Larson**

All rights reserved. No part of this publication may be reproduced, distributed, or transmitted in any form or by any means, including photocopying, recording, or other electronic or mechanical methods, without the prior written permission of the publisher, except in the case of brief quotations embodied in critical reviews and certain other noncommercial uses permitted by copyright law.

Limit of Liability/Disclaimer of Warranty: While the publisher and author have used their best efforts in preparing this book, they make no representations or warranties with respect to the accuracy or completeness of the contents of this book and specifically disclaim any implied warranties of merchantability or fitness for a particular purpose. No warranty may be created or extended by sales representatives or written sales materials. The advice and strategies contained herein may not be suitable for your situation. You should consult with a professional where appropriate. Neither the publisher nor author shall be liable for any loss of profit or any other commercial damages, including but not limited to special, incidental, consequential, or other damages.

ISBN: 9798867536008

DEDICATION

For Corey

TABLE OF CONTENTS

INTRODUCTION 1

MEALS RECIPES 14

    Lean Ground Beef And Veggies 15

    Beef Stew 16

    Skillet Rice And Beef 17

    Chicken, Rice And Vegetables 18

    Turkey With Mixed Vegetables 19

    Slow Cooker Beef, Quinoa And Beans 20

    Turkey, Beef And Vegetables 21

    Turkey And Rice Buggers 22

    Slow Cooker Chicken And Rice 23

    Salmon And Potato 24

    Salmon, Sweet Potato And Veggies 25

    Salmon And Quinoa 26

    Stovetop Turkey And Veggies 27

    Doggie Omelet 28

    Slow Cooker Pork And Sweet Potato 29

    Pork And Beef Liver 30

    Turkey And Rice Casserole 31

    Beef Casserole 32

    Slow Cooker Chicken Stew 33

    Beef Liver And Chicken 34

    Turkey And Cauliflower Meal 35

    Turkey Stew 36

- Turkey, Rice And Carrot 37
- Rosemary Beef 38
- Turkey Macaroni 39
- Pork And Butternut Squash 40
- Turkey And Beef Meatloaf 41
- Chicken Risotto 43
- Lamb And Oatmeal Meatloaf 44
- Beef And Butternut Squash Stew 45
- Mushroom Soup 46
- Slow Cooker Beef And Kidney Beans 47
- Turkey Mince And Couscous 48
- Spinach Frittata 49
- Beef And Chickpea Meal 50
- Chicken And Lentils Meal 51
- Chicken, Rice And Beans 52
- Beef And Potato Patties 53
- Chicken And Potato Patties 54
- Mozzarella Beef Liver Quiche 55

RAW MEALS RECIPES 57
- Ground Turkey And Organ Patties 58
- Chicken Thigh And Vegetables 59
- Beef And Sardine 60
- Rabbit And Organ Meal 61
- Beef And Vegetable Burgers 62
- Chicken Neck And Beef 63
- Turkey And Sardines 64

Beef, Chicken Vegetable Medley 65

All Round Raw Dog Food 66

Turkey Medley 67

Chicken And Vegetable Meal 68

Bone-in Chicken And Vegetables 69

TREATS RECIPES 71

Doggy Meatballs 72

Liver Bites Treat 73

Butternut Squash Bites 74

Frozen Yogurt Berry Pops 75

Frozen Cinnamon Yogurt Apple Pops 76

Cinnamon Cookie Treats 77

Turkey Apple Meatballs 78

Roasted Chickpeas 79

Carrot Oat Cookies 80

Apple Oat Cookies 82

Cornmeal Biscuits 83

Peanut Butter Treats 84

Cornbread Balls 85

Carrot Peanut Butter Muffins 86

Banana Carrot Muffins 87

Pumpkin Oat Treats 88

Parmesan Biscuits 89

Blueberry Oat Muffins 91

Pomegranate Oat Cookies 92

Soft Carrot Dog Treat 93

- Almond Biscuits 94
- Whole Wheat Pumpkin Treats 95

CHEWY TREATS 97
- Sweet Potato Chews 98
- White Fish Chews 99
- Chicken Chews 100
- Beef Chews 101
- Apple Oatmeal Chews 102
- Beef Tripe Chews 103
- Dehydrated Banana Chews 104
- Apple Chips 105
- Banana Blueberry Fruit Leather 106

SPECIAL OCCASIONS RECIPES 107
- Dog Birthday Cake 108
- Pumpkin Peanut Butter Cake 109
- Pumpkin Apple Cake 111
- Peanut Butter Banana Cake 113
- Peanut Butter And Carrot Cake 114
- Banana Applesauce Cake 115
- Banana And Apple Cake 116
- Turkey And Carrot Cake 117
- Strawberry Banana Birthday Treats 118
- Thanksgiving Treats 120
- Gingerbread Treat 121
- Easy Cheddar Treats 123

INTRODUCTION

Commercial diet is not something that dogs have lived on for very long. Before pre-packaged food became a thing, dog owners always fed homemade food to their pets. And yes, dogs did well on the food prepared and given to them at home. Many pet owners shared advice about what to give and what not to give dogs. Most of what we know today came from the traditional knowledge of what constitute good diet for dogs. This information has been refined and upgraded by vets and scientist to give us the presently available body of knowledge for homemade dog food. Even with the wide availability of commercial dog food, many owners still prefer to make their dog's food. This is because homemade dog food comes with several benefits.

Benefits of Homemade Dog Food

1. You know the type of ingredients that go into the food. This is especially important for dogs that have allergies and other health conditions. Although some commercial dog food are made for dogs with allergies, you might not always find the one that is a good fit for your pet.

Feeding your dog homemade food may contribute to the prevention of various ailments, including:

Arthritis

Skin rashes and sores

Kidney disease

Allergies

Gastrointestinal problems

Constipation and diarrhea

Upset or frequently sensitive stomach

Diabetes

Obesity

Yeast infections

Liver disease

A simple homemade dog food recipe can provide a solution for addressing potential nutritional deficiencies, such as inadequate essential amino acids from home-cooked proteins or insufficient amounts of calcium, potassium, and magnesium typically found in mineral-rich, dark leafy vegetables.

Providing a well-balanced homemade diet can have a positive effect on your dog's overall health and help minimize the risk of these health issues.

2. You are in control of the quality of the food. Your range of choices include, free-range, organic and more. You can source for fresh food where they have the best produce.

3. Homemade dog food is often a good way to save money on feeding pets. When you buy your ingredients in bulk, you spend less with the added advantage of giving your pet food that is more nutritious.

4. Hygiene and safety. When you are in control of the food making process, you can ensure that the meals are made in a hygienic environment and avoid contamination. Sometimes, commercial dog food recalls happen because some harmful substance got into a batch of the food.

5. Batch cooking helps you to save time. Just like bulk buying, batch cooking dog food and freezing in portion sizes cuts down the amount of time you spend in the kitchen.

Disadvantages of Homemade Dog Food

1. It takes time. No matter how easy or fast a dog food recipe is, it will still take some time to get it ready. You have to buy the ingredients, get them ready, cook and package. You can cut down the time you spend on the entire process by shopping for dog food ingredients when you buy groceries for your family. Also, set aside an afternoon every weekend to batch cook a few recipes.

2. If you don't watch your purse, you can easily spend too much money on homemade dog food. Your dog does not have to eat the same cut of meat that you buy for your family. Cheaper cuts of meat are good enough as long as they are not fatty.

3. Risk of contamination. If you don't observe proper sanitation when preparing and storing dog food, bacteria can easily get in.

4. Risk of nutritional imbalance. Commercially many pet food are designed to provide all round nutrition for pets. This responsibility is on you when you choose to prepare your own dog food at home. This is easily taken care of by feeding your dog different types of meals with a variety of ingredients. This will ensure that nutritional needs are met over time. It is also advisable to give a good multivitamin regularly to dogs on homemade food to cover for any deficiency.

Ingredients In Your Dog Food

When preparing homemade dog food, it's crucial to ensure that it's nutritionally balanced. Balancing ingredients such as protein, carbohydrates, fats, vitamins, and minerals is essential. This is why these foods must be packed with high-quality protein, vegetables, and wholesome grains.

Generally, your dog's food should consist of appropriate portions of important ingredients like eggs, dairy, organ meats, muscle meat or fish, vegetables, and fruits. The proportion used will depend on the ingredients in the food and the meals or recipe you make. Break down these ingredients, calculate the amounts required per meal in order to know how much to feed.

Consider this Basic Guide:

- Muscle meat or fish …… 50%

- Vegetables (Starchy veggies, grains, legumes (beans)) …… 25%

- Dairy (yogurt, goat milk, cheese, others) …… 10-15%

- Organ meats (heart, liver, kidneys) 5-10%
- Eggs ...... Few times per week
- Fruits ...... Small amount

Meats/Fish

You can use a variety of meat proteins to feed your dog, but it's important to ensure they are safe and prepared properly. Some commonly used and safe options include:

<u>Chicken</u>: Skinless, boneless chicken breast or thigh meat is a popular choice. Cooked chicken is a lean source of protein that most dogs enjoy.

<u>Turkey:</u> Lean, cooked turkey meat is another excellent option, and it's often well-received by dogs.

<u>Beef:</u> Lean cuts of beef, such as sirloin or ground beef, can be given to dogs in moderation. Avoid fatty cuts like ribeye or T-bone.

<u>Pork:</u> Lean pork cuts, like pork loin, can be fed to dogs, but make sure it's fully cooked to eliminate the risk of trichinosis.

<u>Fish:</u> Salmon, mackerel, and sardines are rich in omega-3 fatty acids and can be beneficial for your dog's coat and overall health. Ensure

fish is cooked and free of bones. Canned fish in water is also a suitable option.

Lamb: Lean lamb cuts are suitable for dogs in moderation. Like other meats, make sure it's well-cooked.

Organ Meats: Liver and kidney are high in nutrients and can be added in small quantities as a part of a balanced diet.

Ground Meat: Ground meats, such as ground beef or turkey, are easy to prepare and can be mixed with other ingredients for a balanced meal.

Feel free to prepare them according to your recipe's requirements. Numerous canine recipes bear a resemblance to stews or casseroles, making them quite similar to human dishes.

Vegetables & Fruits

Vegetables can constitute approximately 25% of your dog's diet. Opt for nutritious grains like brown rice, oatmeal, barley, amaranth, quinoa, couscous, bulgur, and others, ensuring they are properly cooked. Vary the grains in your dog's meals to provide a range of nutrients for their balanced diet.

High-quality starchy vegetables like potatoes, sweet potatoes, and winter squash are excellent choices. To unlock the nutrients, either puree or steam the vegetables.

For a fruity twist, consider adding apples, papayas, mangoes, berries, or melon to your dog's meals. While some dogs may have personal fruit preferences, always steer clear of grapes and raisins, as they are toxic to dogs.

To ensure a balanced diet, aim to feed your dog 2-3 percent of their ideal body weight daily, divided into morning and evening meals.

Bone Content

Adult dogs require a daily calcium intake ranging from 800 to 1000 mg per pound of food consumed. The calcium should be in proper balance with the phosphorus in their diet, which may vary based on meat consumption.

Dogs eating meat with bones naturally maintain this balance. However, when cooking homemade meals for dogs with fewer bones, it's essential to supplement calcium. Various forms of calcium supplements are available at local drugstores, but it's crucial not to factor in the calcium found in dairy products within your dog's diet.

... In Raw Foods

For bone content in raw homemade dog food, it typically ranges from 10% to 25%. However, a recommended guideline is to aim for approximately 12% to 15% of bone content in your dog's diet. For instance, in a 10 lb. recipe, this would equate to 1.2 to 1.5 lbs of bone. For puppies, it's advisable to provide a slightly higher bone content of 15%.

You have the flexibility to include bone in the form of ground bone added to the food, alternatively, feed raw meaty bones (RMB) to your dog 2 to 3 times in a week as an alternative approach to meeting their bone requirements.

Important Note: Bones should only be included in your homemade dog food recipe if you are making raw food. Bones must never be cooked. For cooked food, bone meal can be used as a suitable bone replacement.

If you opt for bone meal, the recommended amount to feed adult dogs is 2 teaspoons of bone meal powder for every pound of food. For puppies, the guideline varies based on the fat content of the home-prepared food. You can provide 4 teaspoons for every pound of food for recipes with 10% or less fat content, 5 teaspoons per pound for 11 to 15% fat content, or 6 teaspoons a pound for 15 to 20% fat content. Bone meal can also be added to raw food as an alternative to feeding raw bones to your dog.

With all these thoughtful inputs of ingredients and personal care, almost every dog will find it hard to resist meal times.

Determining the Right Amount to Feed

The first step is to determine how many calories your dog needs on a daily basis. This can vary widely depending on your dog's age, breed, size, and activity level. Your veterinarian can help you with this calculation. Once you know your dog's daily calorie requirements, divide the total daily calories into several smaller meals. Dogs typically eat two or more meals per day, depending on their age and preferences.

Here are some general guidelines to determine the right amount to feed your dog:

Adult Dogs: Most adult dogs need to consume approximately 2 to 3% of their ideal body weight a day. This provides a starting point for their daily food intake.

Puppies: For puppies, you can calculate their daily food portion based on either 2-3% of their expected adult weight or 10% of their current weight. It's common to feed puppies three times a day until they reach about 6 months of age.

Adjusting for Activity Level: Tailor the portion size to your dog's activity level. Active and young dogs may require more food, while older or less active dogs might need less. Additionally, adjust the portion size if your dog needs to lose weight or gain it.

Size Doesn't Matter: Homemade dog food is suitable for dogs of all sizes. Just ensure you provide the appropriate quantity based on the individual needs of your dog.

Kitchen Appliances And Tools for Homemade Dog Food

For Raw Foods:

Kitchen scale

Measuring cups

Use a measuring cup or kitchen scale to portion out the appropriate amount of homemade dog food based on the daily calorie requirements. Be precise to avoid overfeeding or underfeeding

Large spoons

Mixing bowls

Cutting board

Sharp knife.

Food Processor (for blending vegetables)

For Cooked Food:

Dutch oven, large casserole or roasting pan, or crockpot.

Storage Or Molding:

Silicone containers

Silicone baking pans or muffin cups

Glass storage containers or storage bags (plant-based eco-friendly).

Note: If using bags, be sure to fill up and, press down flat. This makes them easy to stack in the freezer.

Storing Homemade Dog Food

The shelf life of homemade dog food can vary depending on the ingredients used and how it is stored. Here are some general guidelines:

Refrigeration: If you've prepared homemade dog food and want to store it in the refrigerator, it's best to consume it within 3-5 days. This will help ensure that the food remains fresh and safe for your dog. Be sure to store it in an airtight container to prevent spoilage and contamination.

Freezing: Homemade dog food can typically be frozen for up to 2-3 months. Divide the food into portion-sized servings and store them in airtight containers or freezer bags. Freezing can help preserve the nutritional value of the food and prevent spoilage.

To heat up your dog's homemade meal, just like you do to human food, simply microwave for 15 to 60 seconds depending on the ingredients.

Monitoring freshness: Regardless of the storage method, it's important to monitor the freshness of the homemade dog food. Look for signs of spoilage, such as an off odor, changes in color or texture, or the presence of mold. If you observe any of these signs, throw the food away.

Ingredients matter: The shelf life can also be influenced by the ingredients you use. Fresh, high-quality ingredients are less likely to spoil quickly compared to lower-quality ingredients. Be sure to follow safe food handling practices when preparing homemade dog food to minimize the risk of contamination.

Find healthy recipes below to make those yummy foods and treats for your furry friend. *Happy Cooking!*

MEALS RECIPES

Lean Ground Beef And Veggies

Prep Time: 10 mins

Cook Time: 55 mins

Yield: 4 cups

Ingredients:

1/3 cup brown rice

1 pound lean ground beef

1/3 chopped cup carrots

1/3 cup chopped sweet potato

1 cup green beans

1/4 cup chopped celery

Directions:

1. Follow package instructions to cook the rice.

2. When rice is done, add the ground beef to a large skillet and brown on medium heat.

3. Add the cooked rice and the vegetables to the browned beef. Stir to combine. Set heat to low and cook with occasional stirring for 15 minutes.

Beef Stew

Prep Time: 20 mins

Cook Time: 30

Yield: 4 cups

Ingredients:

1 small sweet potato, cubed

1 pound beef stewing meat, cut into 1-inch pieces

1 tablespoon vegetable oil

1/2 cup water

3 tablespoons flour

1/3 cup green peas

1/3 cup diced green beans

3/4 cup diced carrots

Directions:

1. Add the sweet potato cubes to a saucepan, cover with water and cook on medium heat for 15 minutes, or until tender. Drain and set aside.

2. Meanwhile, add the vegetable oil to large skillet on medium heat. Add the beef chunks and cook, occasionally stirring until done, about 12-15 minutes. Use a perforated spoon to remove the meat and reserve the drippings in the pan.

3. Return the skillet with the drippings to medium heat then stir in the water and flour.

4. Add the meat and the vegetables stirring until well coated.

5. Cook until carrots are tender, about 10 additional minutes.

Skillet Rice And Beef

Prep Time: 10 mins

Cook Time: 50 mins

Yield: 8 cups

Ingredients:

2 cups brown rice, steamed

1/2 cup chopped broccoli

1/2 cup shredded carrots

1 pound ground beef

1 tablespoon vegetable oil

Directions:

1. Follow package instructions to cook the brown rice.

2. While rice is cooking, steam carrots and broccoli on the stove top.

3. Add the ground beef and vegetable oil to a large skillet and brown on medium heat, stirring until done.

4. Stir in the rice, carrots and broccoli. Cook for 5 minutes more.

Chicken, Rice And Vegetables

Prep Time: 15 mins

Cook Time: 30 mins

Yield: 9 cups

Ingredients:

1 1/2 pounds boneless chicken, shredded

2 cups rice

1 1/2 cups frozen vegetable blend, chopped

3 1/2 cups water

Directions:

1. In a saucepan, stir together all the ingredients until well distributed.

2. Bring to a boil on medium high heat with constant stirring.

3. Cover the pan, set the heat to medium-low then allow to simmer for about 25 minutes or until the rice softens and the water is absorbed.

Turkey With Mixed Vegetables

Prep Time: 10 mins

Cook Time: 25 mins

Yield: 9 cups

Ingredients:

2 1/2 pounds ground turkey

1 1/2 pounds frozen mixed vegetables (corn, carrots, green beans etc.)

2 – 3 tablespoons coconut oil

1 1/2 cups bone broth

2 cups cooked oats

1/4 cup plain yogurt, to serve

Directions:

1. In a lager pot, cook the ground turkey, stirring until browned. Drain and discard the grease.

2. Return the meat to the stove then add the vegetables and the oil. Mix until well combined then cook for about 2 minutes.

3. Add the oats, stir and add the bone broth and bring the mixture to a boil.

4. Cover the pot, reduce the heat and let simmer for 10 to 15 minutes, or until the liquid is absorbed.

Slow Cooker Beef, Quinoa And Beans

Prep Time: 10 mins

Cook Time: 6 hours

Yield: 14 cups

Ingredients:

2 1/2 pounds ground beef

1 1/2 cups diced squash

1 1/2 pounds quinoa

1/2 cup peas

1 (15 ounce) can kidney beans (drained, rinsed)

1 1/2 cups chopped carrots

4 cups water

Directions:

1. Add the ground beef to the bottom of a slow cooker, then top with the remaining ingredients adding the water last.

2. Set the slow cooker to low heat and cook for 6 hours. Open the pot occasional to stir the ingredients.

Turkey, Beef And Vegetables

Prep Time: 10 mins

Cook Time: 55 mins

Yield: 12 cups

Ingredients:

8 ounces ground turkey

8 ounces ground beef

1 1/2 cups brown rice

1 cup water

1 1/2 cups chicken broth

2 eggs, beaten slightly

8 ounces baby carrots

1 small baking potato, quartered

Directions:

1. In a large pot, add together the ground meats and cook until browned.

2. Stir in the brown rice, water and chicken broth. Cover and cook for 30 minutes over medium heat.

3. Add eggs, carrots and potatoes then continue cooking for 20 to 25 minutes more. Add a little more water if necessary.

4. Let cool completely before serving. Store extra for up to 5 days in the fridge and up to 3 months in the freezer.

Turkey And Rice Buggers

Prep Time: 15 mins

Cook Time: 35 mins

Yield: 6

Ingredients:

1 cup of brown rice

1 pound turkey mince

1/2 cup of chopped apple

1/4 cup chopped carrot

1/4 cup chopped lettuce

Directions:

1. Follow package instructions to cook the rice. When done, set aside to cool.

2. Preheat your oven to 350°F.

3. In a large bowl, add together the cooked rice with turkey mince, apple, carrot and lettuce.

4. Roll the mixture into a ball then scoop out 1/2 cup measures to make patties.

5. Place the patties on cookie sheets and bake in the oven until firm, about 15 minutes.

6. Let cool completely before serving. Can be kept in the fridge for 2 weeks. Freeze for longer storage.

Slow Cooker Chicken And Rice

Prep Time: 20 mins

Cook Time: 5 hours

Yield: 5 - 6 cups

Ingredients:

500 ounces green beans, chopped roughly

1 cup brown rice

2 cups water

3 carrots, cut into chunks or rounds

1 medium sweet potato, cut into chunks

2 boneless chicken breasts, shredded

Directions:

1. Add the rice, green beans and water to the bottom of a slow cooker then add the carrot, sweet potato and chicken breasts on top.

2. Cook for 5 hours on high.

3. When done, stir everything together and let cool completely before serving.

4. Store leftovers chilled for up to 3 days.

Salmon And Potato

Prep Time: 10 mins

Cook Time: 22 mins

Yield: 5 cups

Ingredients:

2 Yukon Gold potatoes, diced

1/2 cup water

1 tablespoon coconut oil

1 large carrot, shredded

1/2 cup egg whites

8 ounces salmon, canned or raw

1 cup chopped spinach, packed

1/3 cup canned pumpkin

Directions:

1. Add the water and potatoes together in a Dutch oven, cover and cook on medium heat until softened, about 10 minutes.

2. Stir in the coconut oil and carrot then cook for 3 additional minutes.

3. Meanwhile, cook egg whites with a little oil in a skillet until set, about 4 to 5 minutes. 4. Break up the eggs and add to the pot. Stir in the salmon and spinach, cover the pot and cook until salmon is done, about 7 to 8 minutes.

5. Stir in the pumpkin in the last minute of cooking so it can heat through.

6. Let cool completely before serving.

Salmon, Sweet Potato And Veggies

Prep Time: 15 mins

Cook Time: 30 mins

Yield: 9 cups

Ingredients:

1 pound salmon, skin on

1 tablespoon cooking oil

3 sweet potatoes, skin on, cut into chunks

1 head of broccoli, chopped

1 squash, chopped

2 carrots, chopped

Directions:

1. Heat oil in a skillet on medium high heat. Add the salmon and cook 4- 5 minutes on each side, or until done. Remove from heat and shred the fish.

2. Cover sweet potatoes with water in a saucepan and cook until tender. At the same time, steam the broccoli, squash and carrots until soft.

3. Mash the sweet potatoes then mix with the salmon and vegetables. Mix well.

4. Let cool completely before serving.

5. Store extra for up to 5 days in the fridge and up to 3 months in the freezer.

Salmon And Quinoa

Prep Time: 15 mins

Cook Time: 25 mins

Yield: 10 cups

Ingredients:

1 cup quinoa

2 pounds salmon

1 large carrot, chopped

1 small squash, chopped

1 zucchini, chopped

4 tablespoons cooking oil

1 (15-ounce) can pumpkin

Directions:

1. Preheat your oven to 375°F.

2. Add the salmon to a lined sheet pan and bake in the oven for 15 minutes.

3. In the meantime, follow package instructions to cook quinoa.

4. Steam the carrot, squash and zucchini for a few minutes.

5. Add together all the ingredients in a large bowl and mix until well combined.

6. Let cool completely before serving.

Stovetop Turkey And Veggies

Prep Time: 10 mins

Cook Time: 20 mins

Yield: 7 cups

Ingredients:

1 pound ground turkey

1 tablespoon coconut oil

1 cup shredded carrots

1 cup baby spinach, chopped finely

1 large zucchini, shredded

1/4 teaspoon dried oregano

1/4 teaspoon dried basil

Pinch of cayenne pepper

1 egg

3 cups of cooked brown rice

Directions:

1. Add coconut oil to a pot on medium-high heat then add the ground turkey. Cook and stir for about 10 minutes or until cooked through and browned.

2. Stir in the carrots, spinach, zucchini, oregano, basil and cayenne. Reduce to medium heat and cook for 5 to 7 minutes, occasionally stirring.

3. Break the egg on top and mix it around until it is cooked through then tirn of the heat.

4. Stir the cooked right into the hot food until well combined.

5. Let cool completely before serving. Store extra for up to 5 days in the fridge and up to 3 months in the freezer.

Doggie Omelet

Prep Time: 10 mins

Cook Time: 20 mins

Yield: 6

Ingredients:

2 tablespoons milk

3 eggs

1/4 cup cooked chicken, cut in small pieces

1/4 cup of shredded cheddar cheese

Directions:

1. Preheat your oven to 350°F.

2. Grease a 6-pan muffin tin slightly.

3. Whisk the eggs and milk together.

4. Stir in the rest of the ingredients.

5. Scoop equally into the muffin tins.

6. Bake until cooked through, about 20 minutes.

7. Let cool completely before serving. Store extra for up to 3 days in the fridge

Slow Cooker Pork And Sweet Potato

Prep Time: 15 mins

Cook Time: 5 hours

Yield: 5 cups

Ingredients:

1 pound ground pork

1 large apple

1 large carrot

1 large sweet potato

1/2 cup water

Directions:

1. Combine everything in a slow cooker.

2. Cook for 5 hours on low, or until the pork is cooked through and breaks up easily.

3. Let cool completely before serving.

Pork And Beef Liver

Prep Time: 10 mins

Cook Time: 20 mins

Yield: 5 cups

Ingredients:

2 pounds ground pork

1 tablespoon of olive oil

6 ounces beef liver

1 1/2 tablespoon chia seeds

1/2 cup grated zucchini

1/2 cup finely chopped celery

1/2 cup pumpkin chunks

1 teaspoon fresh ginger, grated

1/2 teaspoon turmeric

2 large eggs

Directions:

1. Add the oil to a large pan on medium heat then add the ground pork. Cook and stir for 10 minutes or until cooked through and browned.

2. Add the beef liver and cook for 4 minutes more.

3. Stir in the rest of the ingredients, cover then let simmer for 8 to 10 minutes.

4. Let cool completely before serving.

Turkey And Rice Casserole

Prep Time: 10 mins

Cook Time: 20 mins

Yield: 3 cups

Ingredients:

8 ounces ground turkey

2 teaspoons olive oil

1/2 cup peas (frozen or fresh)

2 cups of water

1 garlic clove, minced

1/8 teaspoon cayenne pepper

1/4 teaspoon thyme

1/4 teaspoon turmeric

1 tablespoon ground flax seed

1 cup cooked rice

1/2 tablespoon bone meal

Directions:

1. Add 1 teaspoon oil to a large pan on medium heat then add the ground turkey. Cook and stir 10 minutes or until cooked through and browned.

2. Add the remaining oil then add the peas, water, garlic, cayenne pepper, thyme and turmeric. Cook and stir for 5 minutes more.

3. Remove from heat then add the rice, flax seed and bone meal. Stir to combine.

4. Let cool completely before serving.

Beef Casserole

Prep Time: 10 mins

Cook Time: 25 mins

Yield: 4 cups

Ingredients:

12 ounces beef stewing meat, cut into 1-inch pieces

2 teaspoons coconut oil

1 cup low-sodium beef broth

1/4 cup quick oats

1 cup chopped vegetables (broccoli, peas, green beans etc.)

Directions:

1. Add the coconut oil to large skillet on medium heat. Add the beef chunks and cook, occasionally stirring until done, about 12-15 minutes.

2. Add the rest of the ingredients, cover and let simmer for 10 minutes.

3. Let cool completely before serving.

Slow Cooker Chicken Stew

Prep Time: 15 mins

Cook Time: 5 – 8 hours

Yield: 10 cups

Ingredients:

1 cup brown rice

2 1/2 cups water

2 cups sweet potato, cubed

2 pounds frozen mixed vegetables (carrots, corn, green beans, peas)

2 large chicken breasts, cut into large chunks

Directions:

1. Add the rice, water and sweet potato to the bottom of a slow cooker then add the vegetables on top and lastly the chicken pieces.

2. Cook on low for 8 hours or for 5 hours on high.

3. Remove from the pot and bring out the chicken and shred. Return shredded chicken to the pot and stir everything together thoroughly.

4. Let cool completely before serving. Store extra for up to 3 days in the fridge or 2 months in the freezer.

Beef Liver And Chicken

Prep Time: 15 mins

Cook Time: 30 mins

Yield: 6 cups

Ingredients:

1 pound chicken breasts, cut into 1-inch chunks

1 sweet potato, peeled, cubed

1 cup instant oats

8 ounces beef liver, chopped

1 tablespoon coconut oil

1 red bell pepper, diced

2 large carrots, diced

Directions:

1. Add the sweet potato and chicken pieces to a large saucepan then cover with water. Boil on medium high heat then lower to medium heat, cover and let simmer until done, about 12 to 15 minutes.

2. Meanwhile, add coconut oil to another saucepan on medium heat then add the beef liver. Cook and stir for 7 to 10 minutes, or until cooked through.

3. Add the oats to a bowl then stir in 1 1/2 cups of boiling water. Cover and set aside for 3 to 4 minutes.

5. Combine everything together and mix well.

6. Let cool completely before serving. Store extra for up to 5 days in the fridge.

Turkey And Cauliflower Meal

Prep Time: 10 mins

Cook Time: 20 mins

Yield: 8 cups

Ingredients:

2 pounds of ground turkey

2 tablespoons beef liver, diced finely

1 cup cauliflower florets

1 cup green beans, chopped

2 medium carrots, chopped coarsely

2 tablespoons vegetable oil

Directions:

1. Steam the vegetables on the stovetop 10 minutes, or until tender. Remove from heat, let cool then chop finely in a food processor.

2. Meanwhile, add ground turkey together with beef liver in a large saucepan. Cook and stir on medium-high heat until cooked. Drain any fat and discard.

3. Combine the vegetables with the meat, add the oil then stir everything together.

4. Let cool completely before serving. Store extra for up to 5 days in the fridge and up to 3 months in the freezer.

Turkey Stew

Prep Time: 10 mins

Cook Time: 25 mins

Yield: 6 cups

Ingredients:

2 pounds ground turkey

8 ounces beef liver

1 sweet potato, peeled, chopped

1 cup green beans, trimmed, chopped

Directions:

1. In a large pot, combine all the ingredients and add water until just covered.

2. Bring to boiling on medium-high heat the lower to medium heat and let simmer for 20 minutes or until cooked through. Stir occasionally.

3. Let cool completely before serving.

Chicken & rice

Turkey, Rice And Carrot

Prep Time: 10 mins

Cook Time: 25 mins

Yield: 3 1/2 cups

Ingredients:

8 ounces turkey, cut into bite size

1 teaspoon vegetable oil

1/2 cup rice

1/2 cup mixed vegetables

1 carrot, chopped

Directions:

1. Follow package instructions to cook the rice.

2. Add oil to a pot on medium heat. Add the beef then cook and stir until done.

3. Add the carrots, mixed veggies and some water to a saucepan. Cook until carrot is tender. Drain.

4. Combine everything together and let cool before you serve.

Rosemary Beef

Prep Time: 5 mins

Cook Time: 25 mins

Yield: 9 cups

Ingredients:

1 pound ground beef

2 cups rice

6 cups water

1 teaspoon dried rosemary

1/2 pound frozen cauliflower, carrots and broccoli blend

Directions:

1. In a large pot, add together the ground beef, rice and rosemary. Pour in the water and stir, breaking up the ground beef.

2. Bring to boiling on medium high heat then reduce to medium heat, cover and allow to simmer for 20 minutes.

3. Stir in the frozen vegetables then cook for 5 minutes more.

4. Let cool completely before you serve. Store extra for up to 5 days in the fridge.

Turkey Macaroni

Prep Time: 10 mins

Cook Time: 20 mins

Yield: 6 cups

Ingredients:

1 pound ground turkey

1 tablespoon of olive oil

1 medium sweet potato, chopped

1/2 cup broccoli florets, chopped

1 small zucchini squash, chopped

1 carrots, chopped

1 cup bone broth

8 ounces cooked macaroni

Directions:

1. Heat the oil on medium heat in a pot then add the ground turkey. Cook and stir for about 10 minutes.

2. Add the chopped vegetables and bone broth. Cook until vegetables are tender, about 7-8 minutes.

3. Stir in the cooked pasta and let heat through for about 1 minute.

4. Let cool completely before serving. Store extra for up to 5 days in the fridge and up to 3 months in the freezer.

Pork And Butternut Squash

Prep Time: 10 mins

Cook Time: 17 mins

Yield: 10 cups

Ingredients:

1 butternut squash, peeled, seeded, diced

2 cups of water

2 pounds ground pork

1 tablespoon turmeric

1 pound spinach, chopped

3 cups cooked rice

Directions:

1. Add together the butternut squash pieces and water. Bring to boiling then let cook with occasional stirring until the squash is soft, about 5 minutes.

2. Add the ground pork. Cook and stir until pork is done, about 8 minutes.

3. Stir in the turmeric and spinach. Mix to combine.

4. Stir in the cooked rice, cover and let heat through then turn off heat.

5. Cool totally before serving.

Turkey And Beef Meatloaf

Prep Time: 25 mins

Cook Time: 1 hour 5 mins

Yield: 20 cups

Ingredients:

2 1/2 pounds ground turkey

2 1/2 pounds ground beef

3 eggs

7 potatoes, peeled, cubed

1/3 cup brown rice

4 carrots, finely chopped

2 cups green beans frozen or fresh

3 1/2 cups beef broth

1/2 cup oats

1/4 cup wheat germ

1 (15-ounce) can chopped tomatoes

Directions:

1. In a large pot, combine the potatoes with rice then cover with water. Bring to a boil on medium high heat then reduce to medium

heat and cook until done, about 18 minutes. Drain any water then set aside to cool.

2. Set your oven to preheat to 375°F.

3. In a very large bowl, mix all the ingredients together. With your hands, ensure a thorough mix and get a meatloaf consistency. Add more broth if necessary.

4. Scoop and spread into a large roasting pan (remove the rack).

5. Bake for 40 - 45 minutes.

6. Let cool completely before serving. Store extra for up to 5 days in the fridge and up to 3 months in the freezer.

Chicken Risotto

Prep Time: 5 mins

Cook Time: mins

Yield: 5 cups

Ingredients:

2 cups cooked rice

2 cups cooked chicken thigh meat

3 handfuls spinach, chopped finely

1/4 cup water

Directions:

1. Add all the ingredients to a skillet on medium heat. Cook and stir until heated through.

2. Let cool completely before serving. Store extra for up to 5 days in the fridge.

Lamb And Oatmeal Meatloaf

Prep Time: 15 mins

Cook Time: 40 mins

Yield: 6 cups

Ingredients:

1 pounds lean ground lamb

1 1/2 cups rolled oats

2 eggs

1/2 cup grated apple

1 cup mixed vegetables, grated

3/4 cup diced tomatoes with juice

Directions:

1. Preheat your oven to 350°F.

2. In a bowl, combine everything and mix with hands until you have meatloaf consistency. Add some water or broth if necessary.

3. Scoop into a loaf pan and spread it out.

Bake for 40 to 45 minutes.

4. Let cool completely before serving. Store extra for up to 5 days in the fridge and up to 3 months in the freezer.

Beef And Butternut Squash Stew

Prep Time: 10 mins

Cook Time: 15 mins

Yield: 6 cups

Ingredients:

2 pounds beef

1/2 cup butternut squash

1/2 cup diced sweet potato

1 cup carrot, chopped finely

1/2 cup fresh parsley

Directions:

1. Add butternut squash, sweet potato together with the carrot to a saucepan and cover with water. Boil until softened, about 8 to 10 minutes. Remove from heat, drain and set aside.

2. Meanwhile, add meat to a skillet on medium heat. Cook and stir until browned, breaking up the meat, about 10 minutes.

3. Add the parsley and cooked vegetables to the meat. Mix well then set aside.

4. Cool completely and then serve.

Mushroom Soup

Prep Time: 10 mins

Cook Time: 20 mins

Yield: 3 cups

Ingredients:

1 cup mixed mushrooms

2 cups bone broth

1/4 teaspoon turmeric powder

1/2 teaspoon grated fresh ginger

1/2 cup of fresh vegetables, chopped finely (broccoli, carrot, etc.)

Directions:

1. In a pot, add all of the ingredients and simmer on medium heat for 20 minutes.

2. Transfer to a blender and process to puree.

3. Cool completely and then serve.

Slow Cooker Beef And Kidney Beans

Prep Time: 10 mins

Cook Time: 6 hours

Yield: 12 cups

Ingredients:

2 1/2 pounds ground beef

1 (15-ounce) can kidney beans, drained, rinsed

1 1/2 cups brown rice

1/2 cup peas

1 1/2 cups chopped carrots

1 1/2 cups chopped butternut squash

4 cups water

Directions:

1. In a 6-qt slow cooker, add all the ingredients and pour in the water.

2. Cover and cook for 2-3 hours on high heat or 5-6 hours on low heat. Stir occasionally.

3. Cool completely and then serve.

Turkey Mince And Couscous

Prep Time: 5 mins

Cook Time: 30 mins

Yield:

Ingredients:

3 pounds turkey mince

1 tablespoon vegetable oil

2 cups bone broth

1 cup mixed vegetables (beans, carrots, broccoli)

1/2 cup peaches, peeled, chopped, pureed

1 tablespoon turmeric

Pinch of cinnamon

2/3 cup couscous

Directions:

1. Add vegetable oil to a large pot on medium-high heat then add the turkey mince. Cook and stir for about 10 minutes or until cooked through and browned.

2. Add the peach puree, turmeric and cinnamon. Bring to boiling then simmer on low heat for 10 to 15 minutes.

3. Meanwhile, follow packet instructions to cook the couscous.

4. Add the couscous with the meat and stir to combine.

5. Cool completely and then serve.

Spinach Frittata

Prep Time: 15 mins

Cook Time: 15 mins

Yield: 4

Ingredients:

4 eggs, whisked

1 cup carrots, chopped finely

1 cup spinach, chopped finely

1 teaspoon olive oil

Directions:

1. Heat the oil on medium heat in a skillet then add the carrots and spinach. Cook with stirring until softened. Set aside to cool.

2. Preheat your oven to 350°F.

3. When the vegetables have cooled, mix together with the eggs.

4. Oil muffin pans and scoop the mixture into them to 3/4 full.

5. Bake for 10-15 minutes.

6. Let cool completely before serving.

Beef And Chickpea Meal

Prep Time: 25 mins, plus soaking time

Cook Time: 45 mins

Yield: 16 cups

Ingredients:

2 1/2 pounds chickpeas

3 pounds ground beef or turkey

3 tablespoons canola oil

10 carrots, diced

4 eggs, whisked

4 egg shells, ground

Directions:

1. In a large container, cover chickpeas with 3 to 4 inches of water then soak overnight or for at least 8 hours.

2. Transfer chickpeas to a pot and cover with at least 2 inches of water. Boil then cook on medium heat for 20 to 25 minutes.

3. After the first 10 minutes, add the diced carrots. When done, remove from heat and set aside.

4. Heat the oil on medium heat in a large skillet then add the ground beef. Cook with occasional stirring until cooked through, about 10 minutes.

5. Coat a skillet with oil, add the eggs and scrabble medium heat.

6. Grind the egg shells in a food processor.

7. In a large container, mix everything together until well combined.

8. Cool completely and then serve. Store extra for up to 7 days in the fridge and up to 3 months in the freezer.

Chicken And Lentils Meal

Prep Time: 5 mins

Cook Time: 25 mins

Yield: 9 cups

Ingredients:

3 1/2 cups water

1 1/2 cups green or brown lentils, rinsed

1 large sweet potato, peeled, chopped finely

2 carrots, chopped finely

2 pounds ground chicken

1 tablespoon olive oil, or more

2 1/2 cups spinach

Directions:

1. In a saucepan, add together water and lentils. Bring to boiling then cover and allow to simmer until the water is completely absorbed, about 20 to 25 minutes. The lentils should be cooked by then.

2. Add oil to a large pot on medium heat and then place in the ground chicken. Cook and stir for about 10 minutes or until cooked through and browned.

3. Add the sweet potato, carrots and spinach. Cook and stir for 5 minutes more. Add more olive oil if required.

4. Add the cooked lentils. Stir well and let heat through.

5. Cool completely and then serve. Store extra for up to 7 days in the fridge and up to 3 months in the freezer.

Chicken, Rice And Beans

Prep Time: 10 mins

Cook Time: 45 mins

Yield: 12 cups

Ingredients:

2 cups chicken pieces

1 (15-ounce) can beans, drained and rinsed

1 1/2 cups brown rice

1 cup peas, canned or frozen

1 1/2 cups, chopped carrots

1/2 cup green lentils

4 cups water

Directions:

1. In a large pot, add together all the ingredients.

2. Cover and let it boil on medium heat.

3. Reduce to a simmer and cook until rice is softened, about 40 to 45 minutes. Add more water if necessary.

4. Cool completely and then serve.

Beef And Potato Patties

Prep Time: 15 mins

Cook Time: 25 mins

Yield: 6 cups

Ingredients:

2 large Yukon Gold Potatoes, peeled, diced

2 large carrots, diced

1 pound ground beef

1 tablespoon vegetable oil

1/2 cup green peas, shelled

1/4 cup water

1 cup shredded cheddar cheese

Directions:

1. Add diced potatoes to a large pot, cover with boiling water. Cover and cook for 10 to 12 minutes or until the potatoes are fork tender. Drain and mash the potatoes.

2. Meanwhile, heat the oil in a large pan on medium heat then add the ground beef. Cook and stir for 5 minutes.

3. Add the carrots and green peas. Let it cook for 10 minutes while stirring then remove from heat.

4. Add the mashed potatoes, cheese and water. Mix well, adding more water if too dry then set aside to cool for several minutes.

5. Scoop 1 or 1/2 cupful of the mixture and shape into a patty. Continue until you have done all.

7. Wrap each patty in plastic wrap and store in the fridge. When ready to serve, crumble the patty in your dog's serving bowl.

Chicken And Potato Patties

Prep Time: 20 mins

Cook Time: 15 mins

Yield: 3 cups

Ingredients:

2/3 cup grated carrot

6 ounces chicken

4 tablespoons powdered milk

1 cup instant potato flakes

Directions:

1. Set your oven to preheat to 350°F. Place parchment paper on a baking sheet.

2. Add the chicken and meat to a food processor then process until pureed. Transfer to a bowl.

3. Add the powdered milk and potato flakes. Mix until well combined.

4. Scoop a small portion of the mixture, roll into a ball, press into a patty and place on the baking sheet. Continue until you have done all.

5. Bake until firm, about 15 minutes.

6. Cool completely and then serve. Store extra for up to 12 days in the fridge.

Mozzarella Beef Liver Quiche

Prep Time: 15 mins

Cook Time: 20 mins

Yield: 12

Ingredients:

1/2 pound beef liver, cooked, chopped

1 carrot, grated

1/2 cup chopped spinach

6 eggs

1/4 cup shredded mozzarella cheese

1 teaspoons fresh rosemary, finely chopped

Directions:

1. Preheat your oven to 325°F. Spray olive oil spray on muffin tins.

2. Add all the ingredients to a large bowl then mix together.

3. Fill muffin cups about half way then place in the oven.

4. Bake for 20 minutes, or until set in the middle.

RAW MEALS RECIPES

Ground Turkey And Organ Patties

Prep Time: 25 mins

Cook Time: mins

Yield: 6 cups

Ingredients:

2 1/2 pounds ground turkey

4 ounces chicken livers

1/2 cup baby spinach, finely chopped

1 carrot, finely chopped

1 small apple, cored, finely chopped

1 tablespoon ground flaxseed

2 whole eggs (with shell)

1 tablespoon olive oil

1/2 cup plain yogurt

Directions:

1. Place parchment paper on a baking sheet.

2. Add the spinach, carrot and apple to a food processor and process.

3. Add the chicken livers, whole eggs, olive oil and yogurt. Process to combine.

4. Transfer the mixture into a large bowl, add the ground turkey and mix well.

5. Scoop half-cup portions and use your hands to form into patties. Place the patties on the lined baking sheet.

6. Place in the freezer to set then store in re-sealable bag in the freezer.

8. Thaw overnight in the refrigerator before feeding.

Chicken Thigh And Vegetables

Prep Time: 25 mins

Cook Time: mins

Yield: 3 cups

Ingredients:

1 bone-in chicken thigh

1 cup ground beef

1 ounce chicken liver

1 small apple, cored

1/2 cup dog friendly vegetables

1 egg, with shell

Directions:

1. In a food processor, process the chicken thigh, chicken liver, apple and vegetables until finely chopped.

2. Add the ground beef and egg. Process to combine.

Beef And Sardine

Prep Time: 30 mins

Cook Time: mins

Yield: 10 to 11 cups

Ingredients:

3 pounds of lean ground beef

1 bone-in chicken thigh

4 ounces beef liver

8 ounces canned sardines in water, drained, broken apart

2 teaspoons kelp powder

2 teaspoons ground ginger

1/2 cup hemp seeds

4 eggs (with shells)

1/2 cup red bell pepper

1/2 cup spinach

1/2 cup broccoli

Directions:

1. In a food processor, combine the chicken thigh, beef liver, eggs, bell pepper and broccoli. 2. Process until finely chopped then transfer to a large bowl.

3. Add ground beef, sardines, kelp powder, ginger and hemp seeds. Mix together thoroughly.

4. Divide into portion sizes and freeze until needed.

Rabbit And Organ Meal

Prep Time: 25 mins

Cook Time: mins

Yield: 11 cups

Ingredients:

3 pounds ground rabbit

1/4 pound beef liver

1 pound chicken heart

4 eggs (with shells)

1 large apple, cored

1 cup broccoli

1/2 cup spinach

1 teaspoon kelp powder

Directions:

1. Cut the beef liver and chicken heart into small pieces.

2. In a food processor, process the eggs, apple, broccoli and spinach until pureed.

3. Combine all the ingredients in a large bowl and mix well.

4. Divide into portion sizes and freeze in air-tight containers.

Beef And Vegetable Burgers

Prep Time: 25 mins

Cook Time: mins

Yield: 16 cups

Ingredients:

4 1/2 pounds lean ground beef

1 pound beef liver

1 pound beef heart

1 pound vegetables (spinach, broccoli etc.)

1/4 cup seaweed powder

1 cup ground flaxseed

2 teaspoons fish oil

Directions:

1. Place parchment paper on a baking sheet.

2. In a food processor combine the beef liver, beef heart and vegetables. Process until pureed then transfer to a large bowl.

3. Add the rest of the ingredients and mix well.

4. Scoop half-cup portions and use your hands to form into patties. Place the patties on the lined baking sheet.

6. Place in the freezer to set then store in re-sealable bag in the freezer.

Chicken Neck And Beef

Prep Time: 40 mins

Cook Time: mins

Yield: 22 cups

Ingredients:

3 pounds skinless chicken necks

2 pounds lean beef

1 pound beef heart

1 pound chicken heart

1 pound beef liver

10 eggs, without shells

12 ounces mixed berries

8 ounces baby spinach

8 ounces broccoli

8 ounces kale

1 tablespoons of green-lipped mussel powder

3 tablespoons of hemp seeds

1/2 teaspoon salt

Directions:

1. Grind all the meat in a meat grinder then transfer to a large bowl. If using a food processor, cut up the meat first.

2. Process the rest of the ingredients.

3. Combine everything and mix thoroughly.

4. Divide into portion sizes and freeze until needed.

Turkey And Sardines

Prep Time: 25 mins

Cook Time: mins

Yield: 4 cups

Ingredients:

14 ounces ground turkey

2 ounces beef liver

1/2 can of sardines in water, drained, broken apart

1 egg, with shell

1 cup mixed vegetables (bell pepper, spinach, broccoli)

2 teaspoon of hemp seed oil

1/2 teaspoon of kelp powder

1/2 teaspoon of ground ginger

Directions:

1. In a food processor or blender, process together the beef liver and vegetables until pureed.

2. Mix together in a bowl, the ground turkey, sardines, hemp seed oil, kelp powder and ground ginger.

3. Add the pureed veggies and beef liver then mix well.

4. Divide into portion sizes and freeze until needed.

Beef, Chicken Vegetable Medley

Prep Time: 35 mins

Cook Time: mins

Yield: 16 cups

Ingredients:

3 pounds ground beef

1 pound beef liver

1 pound chicken heart

1 pound spinach, chopped

1 pound broccoli, chopped

1 pound mixed berries

Water

Directions:

1. Add the beef liver and chicken heart to and chop them finely.

2. Combine spinach, broccoli and berries in the food processor and puree, adding water as required.

3. In a large bowl, add everything together and mix very well.

4. Divide into containers in portion sizes then store in the freezer.

All Round Raw Dog Food

Prep Time: 45 mins

Cook Time: mins

Yield: 14 -15 cups

Ingredients:

2 1/2 pounds ground turkey

14 pounds chicken neck

1 1/2 pounds beef green tripe

6 ounces beef kidney

6 ounces beef liver

12 ounces canned sardines in water, drained, broken apart

6 ounces spinach

6 ounces blueberries

Directions:

1. Grind the chicken necks in a grinder or chop them up as small as you can.

2. Puree the fruits, vegetables and organ meat, adding water if necessary.

3. In a very large bowl, add everything together and mix very well.

4. Divide into containers in portion sizes then store in the freezer.

Turkey Medley

Prep Time: 35 mins

Cook Time: mins

Yield: 22 cups

Ingredients:

5 pounds ground turkey

2 pounds turkey giblets

1 teaspoon dried rosemary

1 pound mixed berries

1 pound carrots

1 pound broccoli

Directions:

1. Process the organ meat using a food processor then transfer to a large bowl.

2. Puree the berries, carrots and broccoli in the food processor and add to the turkey giblets.

3. Add the ground turkey and rosemary then mix well.

4. Divide into containers in portion sizes then store in the freezer.

Chicken And Vegetable Meal

Prep Time: 35 mins

Cook Time: mins

Yield: 13 cups

Ingredients:

3 pounds chicken breast

2 pounds chicken giblets

2 cups chopped spinach

1 large apple, cored, chopped

1 teaspoon dried parsley

1 tablespoon olive oil

Directions:

1. Process chicken breast and chicken giblets. Transfer to a large bowl.

2. Process the spinach and apple tp puree.

3. Add everything together and mix very well.

4. Divide into containers in portion sizes then store in the freezer.

Dog meat organs & veggies

Bone-in Chicken And Vegetables

Prep Time: 30 mins

Cook Time: mins

Yield: 3 cups

Ingredients:

1 pound, bone-in, skin-on chicken leg quarter

3 ounces chicken livers

1/2 cup pureed veggies (carrots, broccoli, spinach or peas)

1/4 cup plain yogurt

1 tablespoon fish oil

Directions:

1. Grind the chicken then puree the vegetables.

2. Mix all together with the yogurt and fish oil.

TREATS RECIPES

Doggy Meatballs

Prep Time: 10 mins

Cook Time: 20 mins

Yield: 14 - 16

Ingredients:

1 pound of ground beef

1/2 cup almond flour

1/4 cup low fat yogurt

1/4 cup unsweetened applesauce

1 tablespoon chopped parsley

Directions:

1. Set your oven to preheat to 350°F. Place parchment paper on a baking sheet.

2. In a large bowl, mix together all of the ingredients. Mix until well combined.

3. Form into meatballs and arrange them on the prepared baking sheet.

4. Bake for 25 to 30 minutes.

5. Let cool completely before serving. Store extra for up to 5 days in the fridge and up to 3 months in the freezer.

Liver Bites Treat

Prep Time: 10 mins

Cook Time: 30 mins

Yield: 40 to 50 pieces

Ingredients:

1 3/4 cups whole wheat flour

1 pound beef liver, rinsed cut into chunks

1 egg

1/2 cup water

Directions:

1. Set your oven to preheat to 350°F. Spray cooking spray on a rimmed cookie sheet.

2. In a blender, process the liver until as smooth as possible. Transfer to a mixing bowl.

3. Add the flour, egg and water mix until well combined.

4. Scoop the mixture unto the cookie sheet and spread it out evenly.

5. Bake 30 minutes in the oven.

6. Let cool completely then cut into preferred treat size.

Butternut Squash Bites

Prep Time: 10 mins

Cook Time: 50 mins

Yield: 45 - 50

Ingredients:

1 cup butternut squash, cut in half

1 1/2 cups oats, ground

2 tablespoons ground pumpkin seeds

2 tablespoons ground flax seeds

1/4 cup natural peanut butter

1/4 teaspoon cinnamon

Directions:

1. Set your oven to preheat to 350°F.

2. Place the butternut squash in the oven and bake for 25 to 30 minutes. Take out from the oven and set aside to cool.

3. Grind the oats, pumpkin seeds and flax seeds.

3. Scrape the flesh of the butternut squash into a bowl then add the rest of the ingredients.

4. Mix together thoroughly and form into a dough ball using your hands.

5. Place the dough on parchment paper and use a rolling pin to roll out to about 1/4-inch thick.

6. Cut out cookie shapes then place them on a lined cookie sheet.

7. Bake until done about 20 minutes.

8. Let cool completely before serving. Store extra for up to 7 days in the fridge and up to 3 months in the freezer.

Frozen Yogurt Berry Pops

Prep Time: 10 mins, plus freezing time

Cook Time: mins

Yield: 10

Ingredients:

1 cup plain yogurt

20 blueberries

10 strawberries, diced

Directions:

1. Place 2 blueberries and a few slices of strawberries in 10 molds of an ice cube tray.

2. Fill up each mold evenly with yogurt then freeze for at least 5 hours.

3. When frozen pop out the treats and transfer to an air tight container.

4. Freeze for 5 months.

Frozen Cinnamon Yogurt Apple Pops

Prep Time: 10 mins, plus freezing time

Cook Time: mins

Yield: 10 servings

Ingredients:

1 cup plain yogurt

2 green apples, cored, seeded, chopped

1/2 teaspoon cinnamon

Directions:

1. Combine the ingredients in a blender and process until smooth.

2. Scoop into ice cube trays or silicone molds then freeze for at least 5 hours.

3. When frozen pop out the treats and transfer to an air tight container.

4. Can be stored for 5 months in the freezer.

Cinnamon Cookie Treats

Prep Time: 5 mins

Cook Time: 20 mins

Yield: 40

Ingredients:

3 cups rice flour (brown is better)

1 egg

2 teaspoons ground cinnamon

1/2 cup water

1/4 cup honey

Directions:

1. Preheat your oven to 375°F. Place parchment paper on a cookie sheet.

2. In a mixer bowl, mix together all the ingredients until the dough is formed. Add more water if necessary to hold ingredients together.

3. Scoop 1 tablespoon of the dough, roll it in your hands then, place on the lined cookie sheet then press it down to about 1/2 inch cookie. Repeat until you are out of dough.

4. Bake in the oven until light brown, about 18 to 20 minutes

5. Let cool completely before serving. Store tightly covered in a jar for 2 to 3 weeks.

Turkey Apple Meatballs

Prep Time: 15 mins

Cook Time: 25 mins

Yield: 14

Ingredients:

1 1/2 cups of baby spinach

1 tablespoon of coconut oil

1 pound ground turkey

1 tablespoon chopped fresh parsley

1 green apple, cored, seeded, grated

Directions:

1. Preheat your oven to 400°F. Place parchment paper on a baking sheet.

2. In a skillet, melt the coconut oil on medium heat then add the spinach. Cook and stir, until wilted, about 4 minutes.

3. In a large bowl, add together the spinach, ground turkey, parsley and grated apple. Use your hands to mix well.

4. Scoop cookie scoopfuls and form into balls. Place the balls on the lined baking sheet.

5. Bake in the oven until cooked through, about 20- 25 minutes.

6. Let cool completely before serving.

Roasted Chickpeas

Prep Time: 5 mins

Cook Time: 30 mins

Yield: 1 1/2 cups

Ingredients:

1 (14-ounce) can chickpeas drained, rinsed

1 teaspoon ground cinnamon

2 teaspoons olive oil

1/8 teaspoon salt

Directions:

1. Set your oven to preheat to 450°F. Place parchment paper on a baking sheet.

2. In a bowl, toss chickpeas with oil and cinnamon. Spread on the lined baking sheet.

3. Bake for 30 minutes.

4. Let cool fully and then serving (you can also throw some in your mouth). Can be store at room temperature for up to 3 days in an airtight container.

Carrot Oat Cookies

Prep Time: 10 mins

Cook Time: 20 mins

Yield: 24 - 26 cookies

Ingredients:

1 1/2 cups shredded carrots

2 cups oats, divided

1 egg

2 tablespoons coconut oil

1/2 teaspoon ground cinnamon

1/2 teaspoon ground ginger

1/4 cup plain yogurt

Directions:

1. Set your oven to preheat to 350°F. Place parchment paper on a baking sheet.

2. In a blender or food processor, process 1 cup of the oats to flour consistency.

3. Add together in a large bowl, the oats (whole and flour) with the rest if the ingredients.

4. Mix together until you have cookie dough consistency. Add more yogurt or flour as required.

5. On a floured surface, roll out the dough to about 1/4-inch. Use a cookie cutter to cut out cookie shapes and place on the lined baking sheet.

6. Bake in the oven for 20 to 22 minutes.

7. Let cool completely before serving. Store extra airtight for up to 2 weeks in the fridge.

Apple Oat Cookies

Prep Time: 10 mins

Cook Time: 18 mins

Yield: 24 - 26

Ingredients:

3 cups oats, ground

2 cups spinach chopped

2 apples, cored, seeded, grated

2 tablespoons honey

Directions:

1. Process half of the oats to flour in a food processor.

2. Preheat your oven to 350°F.

3. In a large bowl, add together oat flour, whole oats, grated apple, spinach and honey.

4. Mix until well combined. If necessary, add a little water or more oats flour to get cookie dough consistency.

5. Roll out the dough on a floured surface to about 1/4-inch. Use a cookie cutter to cut out cookie shapes and place on the lined baking sheet.

6. Bake in the oven for 15 to 18 minutes.

7. Let cool completely before serving. Store extra airtight for up to 2 weeks in the fridge.

Cornmeal Biscuits

Prep Time: 10 mins

Cook Time: 25 mins

Yield: 20

Ingredients:

1 cup cornmeal

2 cups whole wheat flour

1 tablespoon salt

1 egg

1/3 cup vegetable oil

1 cup of water

Directions:

1. Preheat your oven to 350°F. Spray cooking spray on a cookie sheet.

2. In a large bowl, mix together all the dry ingredients.

3. Gradually stir in the wet ingredients until combined. Continue mixing until you have a soft dough that is just slightly sticky. Add more flour or water as needed.

4. Scoop teaspoonfuls of the dough, roll into a ball and place on the greased cookie sheet then flatten to biscuit size.

5. Bake for 20 to 25 minutes until firm and browned.

6. Let cool completely before serving. Store extra airtight in the fridge.

Peanut Butter Treats

Prep Time: 10 mins

Cook Time: 35 mins

Yield: 24

Ingredients:

1 cup plain oats

1 cup boiling water

5 tablespoons unsalted butter, softened

1 1/4 cup all-purpose flour

1/2 cups corn meal

1 egg

1 cup natural peanut butter

1/2 cup milk

Directions:

1. Preheat your oven to 325°F. Place parchment paper on a cookie sheet.

2. Mix together the boiling water with oats and butter in a large bowl. Set aside for 15 minutes.

3. Stir flour, corn meal, egg and peanut butter. Mix to combine well then stir in the milk. You should have a smooth and sticky dough.

4. Roll small portions of the dough into balls and place on the prepared cookie sheet.

5. Bake for 35 minutes.

6. Let cool completely before serving.

Cornbread Balls

Prep Time: 5 mins

Cook Time: 20 mins

Yield: 10

Ingredients:

1/2 cup cornmeal

1/3 cup unsweetened applesauce

1/2 cup quick oats

Directions:

1. Set your oven to preheat to 350°F. Place parchment paper on a baking sheet.

2. In a bowl, mix all the ingredients together until well incorporated.

3. Divide into 10 equal portions, roll into balls and place on the lined baking sheet.

4. Bake in the oven for 20 minutes, flipping after the first 10 minutes.

5. Let cool fully before serving.

Carrot Peanut Butter Muffins

Prep Time: 15 mins

Cook Time: 14 mins

Yield: 24

Ingredients:

1/4 cup natural peanut butter

1 large egg

2/3 cup coconut oil, melted

1 large apple, grated

2 large carrots, grated

2/3 cup oat flour

1 cup all-purpose flour

1 teaspoon of baking powder

Directions:

1. Preheat your oven to 350°F. Place paper liners in a mini muffin pan.

2. In a bowl, whisk together the peanut butter, egg, coconut oil, apple and carrots.

3. Add the oat flour, all-purpose flour and baking powder. Whisk until fully incorporated.

4. Scoop evenly into prepared muffin pan.

5. Bake for 12 to 14 minutes. Test doneness with a toothpick.

6. Let cool completely before serving. Store extra for up to 7 days airtight in the fridge and up to 1 month in the freezer.

Banana Carrot Muffins

Prep Time: 15 mins

Cook Time: 15 mins

Yield: 16

Ingredients:

1 banana, mashed

3/4 cup grated carrot

2 cups water

1 egg

1 cup all-purpose flour

2 cups of whole wheat flour

1 tablespoon cinnamon

1 1/2 teaspoon baking powder

Directions:

1. Preheat your oven to 350°F. Spray cooking spray on mini muffin tins.

2. Mash the banana in a bowl then add the carrot, water and egg. Mix to combine.

3. In another bowl, mix together the rest of the ingredients.

4. Gradually stir in the flour mixture into the banana mixture until fully incorporated and you have batter.

5. Fill muffin tins to the top with the batter.

6. Bake until light brown, about 15 minutes.

7. Let cool completely before serving.

Pumpkin Oat Treats

Prep Time: 15 mins

Cook Time: 25 mins

Yield: 24

Ingredients:

1/3 natural peanut butter

2 large eggs

1 cup pumpkin puree

3/4 teaspoon cinnamon

2 1/2 cups of whole wheat flour

1 tablespoon oats

Directions:

1. Preheat your oven to 350°F. Place parchment paper on a baking sheet.

2. In a bowl, whisk together the eggs, pumpkin puree and peanut butter.

3. Stir in the oats, flour and cinnamon, Mix to combine well.

4. Place the dough on a floured surface and use a rolling pin to roll it out to about 1/4-inch thick.

5. Cut out cookie shapes then place them on a lined baking sheet.

6. Bake until golden brown, about 20-25 minutes

Parmesan Biscuits

Prep Time: 10 mins

Cook Time: 30 mins

Yield: 20 - 30

Ingredients:

1/2 cup old fashioned oats

2 cups whole wheat flour

2/3 cup parmesan cheese, grated

2 tablespoon vegetable oil

1/3 cup unsweetened applesauce

1/3 cup water, or more

Directions:

1. Preheat oven to 350°F. Place parchment paper on a baking sheet.

2. Mix together the oats, wheat flour and parmesan cheese in a large bowl.

3. Stir in the vegetable oil, applesauce and water. Mix until you have a batter ball.

4. Place dough on a floured surface and use a rolling pin to roll it out to about 1/4-inch thick.

5. Cut out cookie shapes then transfer to a lined baking sheet.

6. Bake in the oven for 25-30 minutes.

7. Cool completely and then serve.

Blueberry Oat Muffins

Prep Time: 15 mins

Cook Time: 20 mins

Yield: 12

Ingredients:

4 cups oat flour

1 teaspoon baking soda

4 tablespoons coconut oil, melted

1 banana, mashed

1 cup unsweetened applesauce

2 eggs

1 cup blueberries (frozen or fresh)

Directions:

1. Preheat your oven to 350°F and then spray cooking spray on a 12-cup muffin pan.

2. In a bowl, whisk together the oat flour and baking soda.

3. Add the coconut oil, banana, applesauce and eggs. Mix until you have a well-combined batter.

4. Fill the muffin tins evenly with the batter. Divide the blueberries among the muffin cups and press them in.

5. Bake 20 to 25 minutes in the oven.

6. Let cool fully before serving.

Pomegranate Oat Cookies

Prep Time: 10 mins

Cook Time: 15 mins

Yield: 25-30

Ingredients:

1 cup tapioca flour

2 cups oat flour

1 egg

1 tablespoon honey

1 tablespoon coconut oil

3/4 cup pomegranate juice

Directions:

1. Preheat your oven to 350°F. Place parchment paper on cookie sheets.

2. In a large bowl, mix together tapioca flour and oat flour. Mix in the egg until combined.

3. Slowly mix in the honey, coconut oil and pomegranate juice. Add more pomegranate juice or flour to get cookie dough consistency. Knead until firm.

4. Place the dough on parchment paper and use a rolling pin to roll it out to about 1/4-inch thick.

5. Cut out cookie shapes then transfer to the lined cookie sheets.

6. Bake for 12-15 minutes.

7. Let cool completely before serving. Store extra airtight in the fridge or freezer.

Soft Carrot Dog Treat

Prep Time: 15 mins

Cook Time: 20 mins

Yield: 25

Ingredients:

2 cups flour

1 cup oatmeal

2 teaspoons baking powder

1 medium sized carrot, shredded

1 egg

1/2 cup applesauce

1/4 cup milk

Directions:

1. Set your oven to 325°F to preheat. Place parchment paper on baking sheets.

2. Mix the flour, oatmeal and baking powder together in a medium bowl.

3. Add the carrot, applesauce, egg and milk. Mix until well combined, kneading with hands as necessary.

4. Scoop 2 tablespoonfuls unto the baking sheet and press down gently. Repeat until the mixture is finished.

5. Bake 20 minutes.

6. Let cool fully and then serve. Store extra an airtight container in the fridge or freezer.

Almond Biscuits

Prep Time: 10 mins

Cook Time: 22 mins

Yield: 24

Ingredients:

2 3/4 cups almond flour

1/4 cup almond milk

1/2 cup natural peanut butter

1 egg

1 teaspoon ground cinnamon

1 teaspoon salt

Directions:

1. Preheat your oven to 350°F.

2. In a bowl, mix together all of the ingredients then roll into a dough ball.

3. Place the dough on parchment paper and use a rolling pin to roll it out to about 1/4-inch thick.

4. Cut out cookie shapes then place on the lined cookie sheets.

5. Bake until browned slightly, about 18-22 minutes.

6. Let cool fully and then serve.

Whole Wheat Pumpkin Treats

Prep Time: 20 mins

Cook Time: 15 mins

Yield: 30

Ingredients:

2 1/2 cups of whole wheat flour

1 teaspoon of baking soda

2 eggs

1 cup pumpkin puree

1/4 cup vegetable oil

1/2 cup natural peanut butter

Directions:

1. Preheat your oven to 350°F.

2. In a bowl, combine flour and baking soda.

3. In a large bowl, add together the pumpkin puree, vegetable oil, peanut butter and eggs.

4. Add the flour mixture to the pumpkin mixture and mix until combined and forms dough. You may have to knead with hands.

5. Place the dough on parchment paper and use a rolling pin to roll it out to about 1/4-inch thick.

6. Cut out cookie shapes then place them on the lined cookie sheets.

7. Bake 15 minutes.

8. Let cool completely.

CHEWY TREATS

Sweet Potato Chews

Prep Time: 10 mins

Cook Time: 3 hours

Yield: 12

Ingredients:

2 sweet potatoes, washed

Directions:

1. Set your oven to preheat to 250°F. Place parchment paper on a baking sheet.

2. Use paper towels to pat the potato dry.

3. Slice lengthwise into about 1/4-inch thick slices. Arrange on baking sheet without overlapping.

4. Bake for 3 hours, flipping after the first 1 1/2 hours.

5. Cool fully before serving.

6. Store airtight or freeze for longer storage.

White Fish Chews

Prep Time: 15 mins

Cook Time: 6 - hours

Yield: 1/3 - 1/2 pound

Ingredients:

1 pound white fish fillets (cod, sole, haddock etc.)

1/2 cup unsweetened pineapple juice

1/4 cup chopped parsley

Directions:

1. Cut the fish lengthwise into 1-inch strips.

2. Mix the pineapple juice with parsley then add the fish pieces. Shake to coat then set aside in the fridge to marinate for 2 hours or more.

3. Dehydrator: Drain the fish and arrange on dehydrator trays. Dehydrate for 6 - 10 hours. They are done when they easily break in half.

4. Oven: Arrange the fish on oven racks, leave the door opened slightly and dehydrate at 150°F for 10 - 12 hours.

5. Let cool completely and then serve.

6. Store for 3 weeks in airtight container in a dark place or up to 3 months in the freezer.

Chicken Chews

Prep Time: 15 mins

Cook Time: 2 hours

Yield: 25

Ingredients:

1 pound skinless boneless chicken breasts

Directions:

1. Preheat your oven to 250°F.

2. Cut chicken into 1/4-inch thick strips. Place on the rack of a roasting pan without overlapping.

3. Bake until dehydrated, about 2 hours.

4. Let cool completely before serving.

5. Chill in airtight container for up to 2 weeks.

Beef Chews

Prep Time: 10 mins

Cook Time: 2 hours

Yield: 20

Ingredients:

2 pounds lean beef

Directions:

1. Preheat your oven to 250°F. Spray the rack of a roasting pan with cooking spray.

2. Slice the meat into thin strips. Place on the rack of the roasting pan without overlapping.

3. Bake until dehydrated, about 2 hours.

4. Let cool completely before serving.

5. Chill in airtight container for up to 2 weeks.

Apple Oatmeal Chews

Prep Time: 15 mins

Cook Time: 15 mins

Yield: 50

Ingredients:

1/4 cup diced apple

1 tablespoon molasses

1 tablespoon vegetable oil

2 tablespoons cup water

1/4 teaspoon vanilla

2 cups rolled oats

1 cup flour

1/2 cup water

1 teaspoon cinnamon

Directions:

1. Preheat your oven to 350°F. Grease a baking sheet lightly.

2. In a blender, puree apple, molasses, vegetable oil, water and vanilla. Transfer to a bowl.

3. Add the rest of the ingredients and mix well.

4. Scoop tablespoonfuls of the mixture on the baking sheet and press flat.

5. Bake 15 minutes.

6. Let cool completely before serving. Store extra for up to 2 weeks in the fridge and up to 5 months in the freezer.

Beef Tripe Chews

Prep Time: 20 mins

Cook Time: 13 hours

Yield: 15

Ingredients:

1 pound beef tripe

1/2 cup water

1 tablespoon Greek yogurt

1/4 cup finely chopped fresh cilantro

1 teaspoon finely chopped fresh ginger

Directions:

1. Wash the tripe and use paper towels to pat dry.

2. Cut into 1-inch thick strips and add to a resealable bag.

3. Add the water, yogurt, cilantro and ginger. Shake to coat then set aside in the fridge to marinate 2 hours or more.

4. Remove the beef strips from the bag and arrange on a dehydrator tray without overlapping.

5. Dehydrate at 160°F for 13 to 14 hours.

6. Let cool completely and then serve. Freeze leftovers.

Dehydrated Banana Chews

Prep Time: 25 mins

Cook Time: 3 hours

Yield: 20

Ingredients:

5 bananas, peeled

Directions:

1. Preheat the oven to 210°F. Place parchment paper on a baking sheet.

2. For each banana, slice lengthwise in half and then slice each half a second time lengthwise to make 4 long pieces.

3. Arrange on the lined baking sheet.

4. Bake for 3 to 4 hours, or until dried. Flip after the first 1 1/2 hours.

5. Let cool completely before serving.

Apple Chips

Prep Time: 20 mins

Cook Time: 2 hours

Yield: 20

Ingredients:

2 large apples, cored

Directions:

1. Preheat your oven to 200°F. Place parchment paper on a baking rack.

2. Slice the apples into 1/4-inch thick slices. Arrange on the baking rack.

3. Bake until crisp and dried, about 2 hours.

4. Let cool completely before serving. Store extra for up to 7 days in an airtight container.

Banana Blueberry Fruit Leather

Prep Time: 10 mins

Cook Time: 8 hours

Yield: 40

Ingredients:

1 large banana, peeled, chopped

1 cup fresh blueberries, washed

Directions:

1. In a food processor, process the banana and blueberries until pureed.

2. Spread the puree on the fruit leather tray of your dehydrator.

3. Dehydrate at 145°F for 6 to 8 hours, or until dried and firm.

4. Let cool completely then cut into pieces.

5. Store extra in the fridge in an airtight container.

SPECIAL OCCASIONS RECIPES

Dog Birthday Cake

Prep Time: 5 mins

Cook Time: 25 mins

Yield: 1 (8-inch) cake

Ingredients:

1 cup flour

1/2 teaspoon of baking soda

1/2 cup pure pumpkin puree

1/2 cup unsweetened applesauce

1/4 cup natural peanut butter

1/8 cup of vegetable oil

1 egg, whisked slightly

Frosting:

1/4 cup natural peanut butter

1/2 cup plain yogurt

Directions:

1. Preheat your oven to 350°F. Grease an 8" round cake pan.

2. Mix together flour and baking soda in a bowl.

3. In another bowl, mix together the pumpkin puree, applesauce, peanut butter and vegetable oil. Add the egg and mix it in until fully combined.

4. Add together the wet ingredients to flour mixture and mix ubtil well combined.

5. Scoop the batter into the pan.

6. Bake until it passes toothpick test, about 25-30 minutes.

7. Transfer to wire rack and let cool completely.

8. To make the frosting, simply mix together yogurt and peanut butter then spread on the cake.

9. Refrigerate left overs.

Pumpkin Peanut Butter Cake

Prep Time: 10 mins

Cook Time: 30 mins

Yield: 2 (6-inch) cakes

Ingredients:

1 1/2 cups oat flour

1/2 teaspoon cinnamon

1/2 teaspoon of baking powder

1/2 cup of unsweetened applesauce

1 teaspoon of baking soda

3/4 cup pumpkin puree

1/4 cup natural creamy peanut butter (unsweetened)

2 eggs

Frosting:

1/2 cup natural creamy peanut butter (unsweetened)

1 cup plain yogurt

Directions:

1. Preheat your oven to 350°F. Spray oil cooking spray on two 6-inch round cake pans.

2. In a bowl, combine applesauce, pumpkin puree, peanut butter and eggs until well combined.

3. In another bowl, mix the flour, cinnamon, baking powder and baking soda.

4. Gradually stir the flour mixture into the wet mixture until fully combined.

5. Scoop the batter evenly into the prepared cake pans.

6. Bake until it passes toothpick test, about 30-35 minutes.

7. Let cool completely on a rack.

8. Make the frosting by mixing together the peanut butter and yogurt. Brush on the cake. You could also garnish with a few dog treats.

Pumpkin Apple Cake

Prep Time: 20 mins

Cook Time: 25 mins

Yield: 2 (6-inch) cakes

Ingredients:

1 cup of whole wheat flour

1 teaspoon of baking soda

1/4 cup natural creamy peanut butter

2 tablespoons vegetable oil

1/2 cup of pumpkin puree

1/2 cup plain applesauce

1 egg

3 tablespoons milk

1 apple, peeled, cored, grated

Frosting:

1/2 cup natural creamy peanut butter

1 cup plain yogurt

Directions:

1. Preheat your oven to 350°F. Spray oil cooking spray on two 6-inch round cake pans.

2. In a bowl, mix together peanut butter, vegetable oil, pumpkin puree, applesauce, eggs, milk and apple until well combined.

3. In another bowl, mix the flour and baking soda.

4. Gradually stir the flour mixture into the wet mixture until fully combined.

5. Scoop the batter equally into the cake pans.

6. Bake until it passes toothpick test, about 24-28 minutes.

7. Let cool completely on a rack.

8. Make the frosting by mixing together the peanut butter and yogurt. Brush on the cake. You could also garnish with a few dog treats.

Peanut Butter Banana Cake

Prep Time: 20 mins

Cook Time: 25 mins

Yield: 1 (8-inch) cake

Ingredients:

2 bananas, mashed

2 eggs

1 teaspoon of baking soda

1/2 cup natural peanut butter

Frosting:

1/4 cup peanut butter

2 bananas, mashed

Directions:

1. Preheat your oven to 350°F. Spray oil cooking spray on an 8-inch cake pan.

2. In a bowl, mix eggs and mashed bananas until well combined.

3. Add the baking soda and peanut butter. Mix well until smooth.

4. Scoop batter into the greased pan.

5. Bake for 20 to 25 minutes, or until it passes toothpick test.

6. Let cool completely on a rack.

8. Make the frosting by mixing together the peanut butter and mashed bananas. Brush on the cake.

Peanut Butter And Carrot Cake

Prep Time: 10 mins

Cook Time: 24 mins

Yield: 2 (6-inch) cakes

Ingredients:

6 tablespoons natural peanut butter

2 eggs, whisked lightly

1 teaspoon baking soda

1/2 cup shredded carrot

Frosting:

1 1/2 tablespoons peanut butter, softened

1/2 cup plain Greek yogurt

Directions:

1. Preheat your oven to 350°F. Spray oil cooking spray on two 6-inch round cake pans.

2. In a medium bowl, whisk the peanut butter with eggs until smooth.

3. Add the baking soda and carrot. Mix until smooth.

4. Scoop equally into the prepared pans.

5. Bake until it passes toothpick test, about 20-24 minutes.

6. Let cool completely on a rack.

7. Make the frosting by mixing together the peanut butter and yogurt. Brush on the cake.

Banana Applesauce Cake

Prep Time: 30 mins

Cook Time: 50 mins

Yield: 1 (6-inch) cake

Ingredients:

1/2 cup of unsweetened applesauce

1 large banana, mashed

1/2 teaspoon baking soda

3/4 cup wheat flour

Pinch of cinnamon

1/4 cup water

Frosting:

1/2 cup natural creamy peanut butter

3/4 cup low fat Greek yogurt

Directions:

1. Preheat your oven to 350°F. Spray oil cooking spray on a 6-inch round cake pan and line it with parchment paper.

2. In a mixing bowl, mix applesauce and mashed bananas until well combined.

3. Add the baking soda, flour and cinnamon. Mix well until smooth then mix in the 1/4 of water.

4. Scoop batter into the greased pan.

5. Bake for 35 to 45 minutes, or until it passes toothpick test.

6. Let cool completely on a rack.

8. Make the frosting by mixing together peanut butter and yogurt. Brush on the cake.

Banana And Apple Cake

Prep Time: 15 mins

Cook Time: 25 mins

Yield: 2 (6-inch) cakes

Ingredients:

1/2 cup of ground whole oats

1 teaspoon of baking powder

1 medium banana, mashed

1 large egg

1 large apple, peeled, cored, grated

1/4 cup natural peanut butter

Frosting:

2 tablespoons natural peanut butter

1/2 cup plain Greek yogurt

Directions:

1. Preheat your oven to 350°F. Place parchment paper in two 6-inch round cake pans.

2. In a large bowl, whisk together the flour and baking powder.

3. Add the banana, egg, apple and peanut butter. Mix until combined (don't over mix).

4. Scoop the batter evenly into the prepared cake pans.

5. Bake until it passes toothpick test, about 25 minutes.

6. Let cool completely on a rack.

7. Make the frosting by mixing together the peanut butter and yogurt. Brush on the cake. You could also decorate with a few dog treats or pieces of fruits.

Turkey And Carrot Cake

Prep Time: 15 mins

Cook Time: 30 mins

Yield: 2 (4-inch) cakes

Ingredients:

1 cup coconut flour

1 pound ground turkey

1/2 cup grated carrots

2 eggs

1 teaspoon fresh parsley

Frosting:

Plain Greek yogurt

Directions:

1. Preheat your oven to 350°F. Spray oil cooking spray on two 4-inch round cake pans.

2. In a mixing bowl, mix together all of the ingredients. Use hands to ensure a good mix.

3. Scoop evenly into the prepared pans.

4. Bake until it passes toothpick test, about 30 minutes.

5. Let cool completely on a rack.

6. Brush with yogurt and serve.

Strawberry Banana Birthday Treats
Prep Time: 10 mins

Cook Time: 20 mins

Yield: 12

Ingredients:

1 banana, mashed

6 strawberries, diced finely

1/3 cup unsweetened natural peanut butter

1/2 cup old-fashioned oats

1 cup oat flour

Water, as required

Directions:

1. Preheat your oven to 350°F. Place parchment paper on a cookie sheet.

2. Mix together the flour and oats in a bowl.

3. In a bowl, mix together the banana, strawberries and peanut butter.

4. Add the flour mix to the banana mixture. Mix to combine well, adding water as required to get cookie dough consistency.

5. On a floured surface, roll out the dough to about 1/4-inch. Using a cookie cutter, cut out cookie shapes and place on the lined baking sheet.

6. Bake in the oven 20 - 25 minutes.

7. Let cool completely before serving.

Thanksgiving Treats

Prep Time: 10 mins

Cook Time: 20 mins

Yield: 40

Ingredients:

1 egg

1 teaspoon ground cinnamon

2 tablespoon molasses

1/2 cup natural peanut butter

2 cups old-fashioned oats, ground

Frosting:

1/4 cup plain yogurt

3 tablespoons low-fat cream cheese

Directions:

1. Preheat oven to 350°F. Place parchment paper on a cookie sheet.

2. Whisk the egg then add the molasses and cinnamon. Mix well.

3. Add the peanut butter and mix until fuly combined.

4. Add the oats flour and mix until well mixed in.

5. On a floured surface, roll out the dough to about 1/4-inch. Using a cookie cutter, cut out cookie shapes and place on the lined baking sheet.

6. Bake in the oven for 18 to 22 minutes.

7. Let cool completely.

8. Make the frosting by mixing together the cream cheese and yogurt. Drizzle on the cake then set aside to set 2-3 hours before serving or storing.

Gingerbread Treat

Prep Time: 10 mins

Cook Time: 15 mins

Yield: 20

Ingredients:

3 cups of whole wheat flour

1/2 teaspoon of cinnamon

1/4 cup olive oil

2 tablespoons honey

1/2 cup molasses

1 1/4 cups water

1 tablespoon fresh ginger, finely chopped

1/2 teaspoon ground cloves

Frosting:

Plain Greek yogurt

Directions:

1. Preheat your oven to 350°F. Place parchment paper on a baking sheet.

2. In a medium bowl, mix together olive oil, honey, molasses and 1 cup of water.

3. In another bowl, mix together the flour, ginger, cinnamon, and cloves.

4. Add the flour mixture to the molasses mixture. Mix until combined adding as much of the remaining water as required to get cookie dough consistency.

5. On a floured surface, roll out the dough to about 1/4-inch. Cut out cookie shapes using a Gingerbread cookie cutter and place on the lined baking sheet.

6. Bake for 10 to 15 minutes.

7. Let cool completely. Drizzle with yogurt before serving.

8. Store extra frozen for up to 3 months in an airtight container.

Easy Cheddar Treats

Prep Time: 20 mins

Cook Time: 25 mins

Yield: 50

Ingredients:

3 cups whole wheat flour

2 large eggs

2/3 cup water

1 cup shredded cheddar cheese

Directions:

1. Set your oven to 350°F to preheat. Place parchment paper on a baking sheet.

2. In a large bowl, mix everything together until you have a dough.

3. On a floured surface, roll out dough to 1/4-inch. With a cookie cutter, cut out cookie shapes and place on the lined baking sheet.

4. Bake in the oven for 20 to 25 minutes.

5. Let cool completely before serving.

6. Store extra in airtight for up to 6 weeks in the fridge and up to 4 months frozen.

Concluded

www.ingramcontent.com/pod-product-compliance
Lightning Source LLC
LaVergne TN
LVHW021447231224
799792LV00005B/432